THE LITTLE
BOOK OF
IRISH
JOKES

THE LITTLE BOOK OF IRISH JOKES

Copyright © Summersdale Publishers Ltd, 2016

Research by Agatha Russell

Illustrations © Shutterstock

Summersdale Publishers Ltd
46 West Street
Chichester
West Sussex
PO19 1RP
UK

www.summersdale.com

Printed and bound in Malta

ISBN: 978-1-84953-953-1

Substantial discounts on bulk quantities of Summersdale books are available to corporations, professional associations and other organisations. For details contact general enquiries: telephone: +44 (0) 1243 771107, fax: +44 (0) 1243 786300 or email: enquiries@summersdale.com.

THE LITTLE BOOK OF IRISH JOKES

Cormac O'Brien

summersdale

**THERE ARE ONLY TWO
TYPES OF PEOPLE
IN THE WORLD.**

**THE IRISH...
AND THOSE WHO
WISH THEY WERE.**

An ice-cream seller from Cork was found on the floor of his van, covered in pink sprinkles. They say he topped himself.

'I've often thought about drowning my troubles,' said Colin, 'but my wife won't get in the sea with me.'

Two Irishmen saw a sign that said 'Tree fellers wanted'. The first said to the second, 'If Mick were with us, we'd have got the job!'

Owen went to buy a wristwatch. The man in the shop asked him, 'Analogue?' He said, 'No, just the watch, thanks.'

Patrick got to work late. His boss raised his voice, 'You should have been here at 8.30!'

'Why, what happened at 8.30?'

Danny took karate lessons so he could kill a man with his bare feet. Unfortunately, on his way home one night he was mugged before he could get his shoes and socks off.

Coleen: My grandmother started walking three miles a day when she was sixty.

Bridget: Well it's good to stay fit at her age.

Coleen: She's ninety-seven now and we don't know where the hell she is.

THERE WERE TWO
FISH SWIMMING
IN THE IRISH SEA.
ONE SAID TO THE
OTHER, 'I'VE BEEN
THINKING ABOUT
GOING ON LINE, BUT
I'VE HEARD IT CAN BE
QUITE DANGEROUS.'

Connor walks into a bar with an Englishman and a Scotsman. The barman looks up and says, 'What the hell is this? Some kind of joke?'

Shane saw a good offer on hair pieces. He said, 'That's a small price toupee.'

Andrea knew exactly how batteries felt. She was never included in anything either.

'We're a man short,'
said the foreman.

'Why don't you employ
me brother?' replied
O'Shea. 'He can do the
work of two men.'

'Great, send him
in, you're fired!'

Colm: Would you like to dance?

Fiona: Yes!

Colm: Great, I can take this seat then!

A policeman approached Riley holding a really thin piece of paper. He said, 'I want you to trace someone for me.'

Mrs O'Toole asked Finola why she'd written in her essay that bees must have sticky hair.

To which Finola replied, 'Because they use honey combs, Miss.'

Donal: I was watching a charity marathon and do you know what I saw?

Finn: What did you see?

Donal: Well, I saw a runner dressed as a chicken, and then another dressed as an egg. So I thought to myself, this could be an interesting finish.

A corn on the cob walks into an Irish farmhouse. The farmer says, 'Want to hear a good joke?' The corn on the cob says 'I'm all ears!'

**'What would you be
if you weren't Irish?'
asked the barman.**

Pat replied, 'Ashamed!'

**Mary wondered
how the man in the
moon cut his hair.**

Eclipse it.

WHEN I WAS YOUNG
I ASKED MY MOTHER
WHAT A COUPLE WAS
AND SHE SAID: 'OH,
TWO OR THREE.' SHE
STILL WONDERS WHY
HER MARRIAGE
WAS SHAKY.

My wife asked that I try to be a more 'modern man'. So I went out and got her a present.

'Tampons, Diarmuid! That's not a proper present,' she said. So I tried again.

This time I got her a bra. It said on the label: 'The Sheepdog: it rounds them up and points them in the right direction.'

**Doctor: I have bad news
and worse news.**

Eoghan: What's the bad news?

Doctor: You only have 24 hours to live.

Eoghan: That's terrible. How can
the news possibly be worse?

**Doctor: I've been trying to
contact you since yesterday.**

Dana heard that most accidents happened within a two-mile radius of home – so she moved.

It is the skill of an Irishman to be able to argue either side of a question – often at the same time!

Doyle saw an advert for *Mission: Impossible 5* the other day. He thought to himself: 'it's not really impossible if he's already done it four times.'

EGAN THE ODD-JOB
MAN IS USELESS.
I GAVE HIM A LIST
OF JOBS TO DO
AND HE ONLY DID
ONE, THREE, FIVE
AND SEVEN.

O'Leery stood at the altar, swaying from side to side. What a way to be on your wedding day!

'This man is drunk!' said Father Casey to the bride.

'I know, Father,' she said. 'But sure he wouldn't have come if he was sober!'

I've never understood why people say, 'It's always in the last place you look.'

Well of course it is – why would you keep looking for it after you've found it?

'I'm having amnesia and déjà vu all at the same time,' said Shauna. 'It's like I've forgotten this before.'

**Nolan was telling his friend
that he and his wife had a serious
argument the night before.**

'But it ended,' he said, 'when
she came crawling to me on
her hands and knees.'

'What did she say?' asked the friend.

Nolan replied, 'She said, "Come out
from under that bed, you coward!"'

Fintan: Excuse me, landlord, but do lemons have legs?

Landlord: I don't think they do, why do you ask?

Fintan: Well then, I think I've squeezed your budgie into me gin!

McGee had asked
O'Leery for the hand of
his eldest daughter.
'Can you support a family?'
O'Leery asked him.

'Oh yes, I should think
so,' replied McGee.

'Well,' said his future
father-in-law, 'there are
six of us, you know!'

Murphy: Me wife is driving me to drink!

Seamus: You're lucky! Mine makes me walk!

Aiden tried to visit the paper shop – but it had blown away.

Brought up in the courts for drunk and disorderly behaviour, Mickey sits in the dock. When asked, 'What do you have to say for yourself?' he replies, 'Your Honour, it must be said, I was sober enough to know I was drunk.'

My son, Sean, was married yesterday. I heard him tell his bride, Maureen, that his ring was so tight it was cutting off his circulation.

She replied, 'That's what it's supposed to do.'

I MET A MAN FROM GALWAY WHO TOLD ME NEVER TO LAUGH AT YOUR WIFE'S CHOICES...

BECAUSE YOU'RE ONE OF THEM.

A man walked into a bar in Cork and asked the barman if he had heard the latest Kerryman joke.

'I'm warning you,' said the barman, 'I'm a Kerryman myself.'

'That's alright,' said the customer, 'I'll tell it slowly.'

It took Una eight
months to put her
jigsaw puzzle together.
She was boasting
about it because the
box said 3–4 years.

Finnegan: My wife has a terrible habit of staying up till two o'clock in the morning. I can't break her out of it.

Keenan: What on earth is she doin' at that time?

Finnegan: Waitin' for me to come home.

**Did you hear about the
man on a Guinness diet?**

He's lost three days already.

**Why didn't the Irish
lifeguard save the hippie?**

Because he was too
far out, man!

Brian: Frank, why is it that whenever you ask an Irishman a question, he answers with another question?

Frank: Who told you that?

Deedra's therapist told her that the best way to find inner peace was to finish everything she had started. So she went straight home and polished off a bag of jelly babies and a leftover tart.

MURPHY OPENED HIS
PUB FROM 10 A.M. TO
11 P.M. EVERY DAY.
AS HE ALWAYS SAID
AT CLOSING TIME, 'IF
YOU HAVEN'T HAD
YOUR FILL BY NOW,
YOU SIMPLY HAVEN'T
BEEN TRYING
HARD ENOUGH.'

'I'm not sure about this duck hunting. We've been here for five hours and we still haven't caught one,' said Fergal.

'Maybe we're not throwing the dog high enough,' suggested Niall.

Róisín slept in a castle once every two weeks. It was her fort night.

The Kerry farmer thought that the Royal Mint was what the Queen put on her roast lamb.

THE FOREMAN AT THE BUILDING SITE CALLED OUT TO THE ASSEMBLED LADS, 'THE SHOVELS HAVEN'T ARRIVED YET, AND UNTIL THEY DO, YOU'LL HAVE TO LEAN ON EACH OTHER!'

Ryan walks into a fish and chip shop and says, 'I'll have two portions of cod and chips.'

'Coming right up – the fish won't be long,' said the shopkeeper.

'Then they'd better be fat!' replied Ryan.

Two old nuns were sitting in the garden of their convent. Sister Rosemary gazed over the lawns surrounded by pretty flowers and shrubs, then turned to Sister Josephine and smiled: 'The nice thing about being senile is you can hide your own Easter eggs.'

Eila put down the dog last week; she blamed it for digging little holes all over the garden. Then her husband Kenny said, 'Where's the dog? He used to sit on the lawn and watch me play golf.'

Father McPhee walked into the church and spotted a man sitting cross-legged on the altar.

'My son,' said the priest, 'what are you doing? Who are you?'

'I'm God,' replied the strange man.

'I'm sorry?'

'I'm God,' he said again. 'This is my house!'

Father McPhee ran into the presbytery and, panicking, called the archbishop.

'Your Reverence,' he began, 'I'm sorry to trouble you, but there's a man sat on the altar here who claims he's God. What should I do?'

'Take no chances,' replied the archbishop. 'Go back into the church and look busy!'

Emmet: Anyone who can guess how many ducks are in this bag can have both of them.

Dylan: Three!

Emmet: That's near enough.

Ronan: Why did you call your dog 'I-know-what-you-did'?

Derry: I really like how many people jump in the air when I call his name.

Have you heard about the Irish boomerang? It doesn't come back – it just sings songs about how much it wants to.

When the time came for his child to be baptised, Mike Mulligan proudly stood by the font in St Mary's Church.

'Now then,' said Father Carey, 'what are we going to call this little one?'

'Hazel,' said Mulligan, with a smile.

'Lord have mercy,' said the priest. 'All the saints in Heaven, and you're naming her after a nut!'

'SO WHAT DOES YOUR HUSBAND DO?' ASKED MOIRA.

'HE WORKS IN THE CLOCK FACTORY,' REPLIED KATHERINE. 'HE SITS DOWN AND MAKES FACES ALL DAY LONG!'

**An Irish policeman
in Liverpool found a
dead horse in Cazneau
Street. Not sure of
how to spell Cazneau
Street, he dragged the
beast to Hill Street.**

**What's the difference
between a Cork farmer
and a coconut?**

**You can get a drink
out of a coconut.**

**Why did the Irish king
leave his castle and
go to the dentist?**

**To get his
teeth crowned.**

My mother used to tell me, 'Before you assess a man, walk to Tipperary in his shoes.'

'And why's that?' I asked.

'Well after that who cares? He's miles away and you've got his shoes.'

**Maloney was seen trying to shin up a
massive flagpole, with little success.**

'What's the problem?' asked O'Donnell.

**'The boss wants me to measure
this pole,' said Maloney.**

'Well, save yourself the effort and lay the
pole down, why don't you?' O'Donnell replied.

**'No good,' said Maloney. 'He wanted
the height not the length.'**

The waitress at that new cafe in Balbriggan must have written down my order wrong.

I was filled with uncertain tea.

Dermot went to the doctor
for a check-up and was told he had
high blood pressure. 'It runs
in the family,' he said.

'On your mother or father's
side?' asked the doctor.

'Neither,' Dermot replied.
'It's on my wife's side.'

The doctor, confused, asked,
'How can your wife's family give
you high blood pressure?'

Dermot replied, 'You try
spending the weekend with them.'

Frank: I think our son gets all his brains from me.

Shelley: You're probably right. I still have all mine.

Teenager: Mammy, can I please wear a bra?

Mother: No.

Teenager: Why? I'm nearly fifteen years old!

Mother: I won't say it again, Daniel! No!

Teacher: Who gave you that black eye, Shay?

Shay: No one gave it to me, Miss – I fought really hard for it.

On their fortieth wedding anniversary a sixty-year-old couple, Mary and Kenny, were granted two wishes by a fairy who appeared before them. Mary wished to see the world and 'poof', she had tickets for a world cruise. Kenny wished for a wife thirty years younger than him and 'poof', he was ninety.

A man walks into a Dublin pub with a slab of tarmac under his arm and says, 'A Guinness please, and one for the road.'

Ten minutes later, a man walks into the same pub clutching a set of jump leads. The bartender says, 'You can come in, just don't start anything!'

Molly: Doctor, there's a carrot growing in my ear.

Doctor: How did that happen?

Molly: For the life of me, I don't know – I planted cauliflowers.

Why did schoolboy Seamus write on his toes?

He was trying to think on his feet.

Moya goes into a gun shop and asks for a rifle. 'It's for my husband,' she informs the sales assistant.

'Did he tell you what make to get?' the assistant asks.

'Of course not!' replies Moya, 'He doesn't know I'm going to shoot him.'

A young boy from Wexford saved his sister from drowning. When interviewed by the newspapers, he said, 'I wouldn't do it again. She's been a pain this week.'

'What are you getting your wife for Christmas?' Kelly asked O'Keefe.

'She decided for me,' said O'Keefe. 'She wanted something with diamonds in, so I've bought her a pack of cards!'

How did the hipster from Dublin burn his tongue?

He drank his coffee before it was cool.

Seamus: Me boy just got the clock going after nearly thirty years.

Mick: He must have been very young when he started!

Two men sat in a Dublin pub. Hung on the wall was a huge mirror, 14 feet long. Looking around the room, Barry suddenly spotted their reflection.

'Sean, Sean,' he said. 'There's two fellas over there who look just like us!'

'Jesus!' said Sean. 'They're wearing the same sorta clothes and everything. I'm going to have to buy those boys a drink!'

But, as Sean started to rise from his seat, Barry said, 'Sit down, Sean! One of them's coming over here!'

Two French counterfeiters had made thousands of genuine looking notes – €50, €20, €10 – but they always wanted more. Scrambling through the discarded notes that had not passed scrutiny, they came upon a note that was completely perfect – except that it was for €18.

'Never mind,' said the boss. 'We'll unload it when we're over in Ireland.'

So they took the note with them and whilst in Cork, they entered a corner shop to get rid of it.

'Excuse me,' said the boss to the shopkeeper. 'Have you got change for an €18 note?'

'Indeed I have, sir,' said the shopkeeper. 'Would you like threes, sixes or two nines?'

**WHAT DO YOU CALL
AN IRISHMAN WHO
KNOWS HOW TO
OUTSMART HIS WIFE?**

A BACHELOR.

'Why won't you marry me?' demanded Fergus. 'There isn't anyone else?'

'Oh, Fergus,' sighed Deirdra. 'There must be.'

Conor O'Keefe was ill and his young son saw his mother sterilising the crockery that came from his room. He asked his mother what she was doing and she said, 'Daddy has germs and these get on the plates, so I boil the crockery so that the germs will be killed.' Having thought for a while the boy asked, 'But Mammy, wouldn't it be handier to boil daddy?'

An American tourist stood
by, watching an Irish farmer
dig and turn over the soil.
Eventually he called, 'Hey pal,
what's that you're doing?'
'I'm digging up potatoes, sir.'
'Potatoes? Those tiny things?
You call them potatoes? Back
home in Milwaukee we have
potatoes ten times that size!'
'Yes sir. But you see, we only
grow them to fit our mouths!'

Dominic was so excited after reading about waterskiing, that he went looking for a lake with a slope on it.

I heard that Liam's a bit simple. When the local swimming pool asked for donations, he gave them a glass of water.

Doctor: You've nothing to worry about. You haven't got pneumonia. It is only influenza.

Kian: Doctor, please be honest with me. Did you not once treat a man for influenza who died of pneumonia?

Doctor: My dear man. Anybody I ever treated for influenza died from influenza. I do not make mistakes.

Liam O'Reilly lay in hospital, bandaged from head to foot, with just two small slits for his eyes.

'What happened to you?' asked his mate, Hurley.

'I staggered out of the pub and a lorry hit me a glancing blow and knocked me through a window.'

'God in heaven!' said Hurley. 'Thank the Lord you were wearing those bandages or you'd have been cut to pieces!'

Murray rang Aer Lingus and asked how long it took to fly from Dublin to London.

'Just a minute, sir,' said the girl on the desk.

'Thanks very much,' said Murray, and hung up.

A young boy called Dillon walked into a barbershop. The barber whispers to his customer, 'This is the thickest kid in the world. Watch while I prove it to you.' The barber puts a €5 note in one hand and two cents in the other. He calls the boy over and asks, 'Which do you want son?' The boy takes the cents and leaves. 'What did I tell you?' laughs the barber. 'That kid never learns!' Later when the customer leaves, the barber sees Dillon coming out of the ice cream shop. 'Hey son! May I ask you a question? Why did you take the two cents instead of the note?' Dillon licked his cone and said, 'Because the day I take the note the game is over!'

Time traveller Rory was still hungry after his last bite, so he went back four seconds.

Tommy was a mathematician. They wrote on his gravestone:

HE DIDN'T COUNT ON THIS.

**DID YOU HEAR
ABOUT JESUS BEING
ON TWITTER?**

**MIND YOU, HE'S ONLY
GOT 12 FOLLOWERS.**

Niall was getting irate
and shouted upstairs
to his wife, 'Hurry
up or we'll be late.'

'Oh, be quiet, man,'
replied his wife.
'Haven't I been
telling you for the
past hour that I'll be
ready in a minute?'

The phone rang in the hospital. 'Hello,' said a frantic voice. 'It's Cormac Delany here. Can you come quickly, my wife is about to give birth.'

'I see,' said the receptionist at the end of the line. 'And is this her first child?'

'No!' exclaimed Delany, 'This is her husband speaking.'

Liam O'Donoghue had drunk more than enough Guinness and had stumbled out of Finn's bar and into the Sunday afternoon air. As his drunken eyes squinted, an ambulance went by at great speed. Blue lights flashing and siren roaring, it sped up the street, with Liam running after it. A hundred yards, two hundred, three hundred... Almost a quarter of a mile he ran after it until finally, lungs and legs giving out, he fell into the gutter. Then, with his last bit of breath he shouted, 'You can keep your ruddy ice cream!'

I've just been to a very
emotional wedding
in Kilkenny.

Even the cake was in tiers!

What did the Irish
Buddhist say to the man
in the burger van?

Make me one with
everything.

Colin and Desmond were addicted to golf.
Colin was about to take a swing when
he noticed a funeral procession go by.

Colin stopped mid-swing, closed his
eyes and said a quick prayer.

Desmond was truly inspired and
remarked, 'Wow, that was one of the
most beautiful things I have ever seen.'

'Well,' said Colin, 'I was married
to her for over 35 years.'

**WHEN THE GARDA
PULLED EOIN OVER,
HE WAS ASKED
'CAN YOU IDENTIFY
YOURSELF?'**

**EOIN JUST LOOKED
IN HIS MIRROR AND
SAID, 'YES, IT'S ME.'**

Brian was on his way back from work when his wife Cathleen called him.

'Brian dear, please be careful. I heard on the news that there is a lunatic driving the wrong way on the motorway.'

Brian shouted, 'Oh, it's worse – there are hundreds of them!'

Reilly is walking through a graveyard when he comes across a headstone with the following inscription:

HERE LIES A POLITICIAN AND AN HONEST MAN.

'Faith now,' exclaims Reilly, 'I wonder how they got the two of them into one grave!'

Farmer's Son: We got a lecture on Yeats in school today, Daddy.

Farmer: And I suppose, ignorant thing that you are, you didn't even know what a Yeat was.

'What's wrong
with Micky?' asked
Father Donnall.
His wife replied,
'I don't know,
Father. Yesterday he
swallowed a spoon and
he hasn't stirred since!'

If you're interested in finding out more about our books, find us on Facebook at **Summersdale Publishers** and follow us on Twitter at **@Summersdale**.

www.summersdale.com